13 Answers for the 13 Reasons W
Health Resource Guide for Parent
By DeQuincy A. Lezine, Ph.D.

MW00387460

Table of Contents

Introduction 1

Answer 1: Stop the bullying 6

Answer 2: Support after a suicide...12

Answer 3: Mental health screening and treatment.......................19

Answer 4: Help for victims of crime 27

Answer 5: Support for LGBTQ youth 34

Answer 6: Substance abuse prevention and treatment..................42

Answer 7: Counter suicide risk, enhance protection 50

Answer 8: Creative approaches to therapy 56

Answer 9: Awareness and prevention of sexual violence.............62

Answer 10: Promote safe driving..68

Answer 11: Know the warning signs for suicide 74

Answer 12: Help after rape..80

Answer 13: Seek help from school mental health professionals.....86

Cheat Sheet: Key resource sites and phone numbers....................94

About the Author...95

Introduction

By now you've probably heard some things about a television drama series featured on Netflix called "13 reasons why" (13RW). Let me address the first question that probably comes to mind:

What is the main idea of this show?

Clay, a teenage boy, receives a set of 13 audio recordings made by his friend Hannah, just before she killed herself. On each recording, Hannah identifies an experience and person that added to the despair and desperation leading up to her suicide. The show alternates between focusing on what happened with Hannah as described on her tapes, and what is going on in the present for Clay and his classmates. Between Hannah's 13 'reasons' for dying and the experience of the other kids in the aftermath, the series hits many teen mental health topics.

Three common questions

1. Should I let my kid watch 13 Reasons Why on Netflix?

Dr. Michael Rich (Boston Children's Hospital Psychiatry) notes that the intense emotions, adult themes, and dramatic material can be particularly harmful to early teen viewers. The brain's full capacity for thinking things through, planning, and resisting impulses doesn't finish developing until early adulthood. There is a risk that kids, in general, will act on their emotions using less complete information than they would later in life. The show themes are likely to resonate with problems and negative emotions while providing almost no guidance on healthy responses.

Dr. Rich suggests talking to your son or daughter about the themes in the show beforehand and finding out what their friends are already saying about the show. In watching the show together, you can help your son or daughter process the material within the context of your larger range of life experiences. In this book, I'll offer some additional guidance on doing that.

Asked a similar question on a webinar discussion, Dr. Dan Reidenberg (Suicide Awareness / Voices of Education; SAVE) also said that the focus needs to be on emotional maturity more than age. They need to understand the limits of what this fictional drama can teach. The information included in this book was selected to put the issues into the context of "real-world" facts.

2. Why are the suicide prevention experts worried?

To be blunt, some people who are already in distress may take the wrong messages from the show and try to kill themselves instead of seeking help. There are records of media reports and depictions of suicide leading to more people trying to kill themselves. Increased suicide after reporting is most likely to happen when stories aren't careful. When done well, reporting or portraying suicide along with information can help change public misconceptions and encourage help-seeking. The guidelines to the media suggest (**http://reportingonsuicide.org**):

- Don't sensationalize suicide.
- Don't include explicit details on a suicide method.
- Don't make suicide seem like a good thing (glamorizing, romanticizing).

Unfortunately, the 13RW show pretty much does everything that experts advise against doing.

3. So why did Netflix do things the way they did?

They seem to have been more confident in their knowledge of the topic than they should have been. I believe that they had good intentions, but their actual knowledge did not match up to their passion or ambition. To their credit, they have been engaged with the suicide prevention community to some degree in response to the criticism voiced by experts. From what I understand, they also did some consulting with mental health professionals ahead of time, but not with specialists.

What are some of the talking points about 13RW for parents to use that have been recommended by suicide prevention experts?

- This show is a fictional cautionary tale.
- There are healthy ways to cope with the topics in the show.
- Reach out and talk to someone if you need support.
- Suicide is not a typical response to life's challenges.
- There are many effective treatment options available.
- Everyone could do something to help prevent suicide.

Like the experts mentioned earlier, The National Association of School Psychologists (NASP) also encourages parents to be willing to watch the series with kids and have "thoughtful conversations about the show... Process the issues..."

Let's say that all the expert commentary has convinced you to talk about the show with your teen. Do you feel ready for the potentially tough conversations ahead? I'll be honest. I wouldn't have been ready to talk about all the complicated issues that come up in the show when I first watched it, and I'm a suicide prevention specialist.

So, I've done a lot of research to write this book and be like your coach. We'll work through the main topics together so that you can go into those conversations feeling well-informed and prepared.

I see each episode as a question: What could help the characters right now?

After watching the entire season and reflecting on specific concerns and issues, I've come up with at least one mental health resource to recommend in answering that question for each of the 13 episodes.

The 13 Answers

For the most part, in the chapters that follow, here's what you'll find:

1) **Why I picked this topic** from the episode will be briefly noted. I'll do my best to keep "spoilers" to the minimum, but I do want you to know what might come up.

2) **I provide my primary resource recommendation** up front for reference. Based on the research I've done for this book, if I had to pick just one resource to give you, then this would be the one. (Don't worry, I'll point out a few others as well).

3) **Terminology** related to the issue will be pointed out.

4) **The question "How common is this issue** in the real world?" will be addressed with statistics. The show might make some things feel like an epidemic. They probably do that because other places make it seem like those problems hardly ever happen. I'll provide some numbers to give you a more accurate idea about it.

5) **The effects** of the issue will be briefly noted. Knowing the effects that an issue can have on someone's mental and emotional health can provide motivation to talk about it.

6) I'll add some additional points to help with **understanding the issue**.

7) I will provide prompts about incorporating **your experience** as part of the discussion. You can help your son or daughter, and help yourself, by bringing your personal experience into the conversation. I'll help with figuring out how to do that.

8) **The signs or symptoms** to look for will be pointed out. Could this have happened to your son or daughter?

9) I'll also at least help you get started with **what to do** if the issue is something that has affected your teen (or one of their friends), often including some specific tips for talking about the issue with your teen.

Answer 1: Stop the bullying

Why I picked it:

In the first episode, many problems come up, but bullying stands out as a major theme that the show producers highlight. Thus, I've selected that as the start.

Primary resource:

StopBullying.gov is the official US government response to the topic pulling in information from across agencies. Their website includes reports on bullying, cyberbullying, identifying risk, preventing bullying, responding to bullying, and getting help.

Terminology:

There are several forms of bullying, which is unwanted aggressive behavior accompanied by one person having more power than the other:

- **Verbal** bullying includes teasing, name-calling, sexual comments, or threats.
- **Social or relational** bullying is leaving someone out of things, telling others not to be friends with them, spreading rumors, or sharing embarrassing pictures of them.
- **Physical** bullying includes hitting, spitting, tripping, or taking things.
- **Cyberbullying** is the use of technology to bully (e.g., mean texts, embarrassing photos).

How common is bullying?

According to the 2015 School Crime Supplement to the National Crime Victimization Survey (**https://nces.ed.gov/programs/crime/surveys.asp**):

- Approximately one in five high school students reports being bullied during the year.
- Girls were more likely to experience bullying than boys were (23% vs. 19%).
- Of the kids who were bullied, 15% reported that it happened at least weekly.
- Bullying is highest in middle school:

6th grade	7th grade	8th grade	9th grade	10th grade	11th grade	12th grade
31%	25%	22%	19%	21%	16%	15%

Effects of bullying:

As noted by StopBullying.gov: "Media reports often link bullying with suicide. However, most youth who are bullied do not have thoughts of suicide or engage in suicidal behaviors." There is some suicide risk associated with bullying, but it is not due to bullying alone. However, adverse outcomes are related to being a bully, a victim of bullying, or observing bullying.

Bully	Bullied	Bystander
• Substance abuse • Physical fights • Early sexual behavior • Adult criminal behavior • Domestic violence	• Depression • Anxiety • Sleep and eating problems • Missing school	• Substance abuse • Depression • Anxiety • Missing school

Understanding bullying:

Why do kids bully others? Sometimes the person who becomes a bully is well-connected and needs to feel dominant and keep their power. Other times, the person is feeling isolated, depressed and anxious, and may be trying to compensate for low self-esteem. Some are aggressive or frustrated. Many are lacking parental involvement.

Why do some kids get bullied? Mostly kids become the target if a bully perceives them as:

- Different particularly by their appearance.
- Seeming depressed or anxious.
- Being less popular.
- Having fewer friends.

Why don't kids report it all the time? Of those who were bullied, the youth notified an adult only 43% of the time. Many students feel like they should be able to handle the issue on their own. Some fear backlash from the bully. Many believe that the experience is humiliating and don't want to share it with anybody else. Some fear that nobody cares at all. And others fear peer rejection if they tell adults about bullying.

Your experience:

The chances are that you have some experience with the topic of bullying on one side or another. Did you get teased or bullied as a kid? You can probably remember what it felt like at the time. You also know how your feelings have changed over time. Think about how you handled it at the time, and what you might change about what you did. Even if you don't have experience with a particular type of bullying, being able to talk about your inner experience, and processing since then, will be a valuable addition to a discussion with your son or daughter.

Did you ever teaser bully someone else? You can probably remember why you picked a certain person, and why you did or said certain things. Again, you also know what has changed for you over time, and what you might do differently. That insight into "why kids would do that" is valuable.

I know it could be embarrassing to tell your son or daughter that someone bullied you, or that you bullied someone else. It's okay to just talk about it as "I knew someone who…" How much you choose to reveal might depend on the circumstances, but being willing to speak from experience can open doors.

Signs of bullying:

They might be bullying others if they:	They might be the target of bullying if they:
<ul><li>Get into fights often.</li><li>Are sent to the principal's office or detention.</li><li>Have unexplained extra money.</li><li>Blame others for their problems.</li><li>Are competitive and worried about reputation or popularity.</li></ul>	<ul><li>Frequently have headaches or stomachaches.</li><li>Have unexplained injuries.</li><li>Frequently fake sick to get out of school.</li><li>Have changes in eating habits such as skipping or binging meals.</li><li>Experience nightmares.</li><li>Start having worse grades.</li><li>Suddenly lose friends.</li><li>Avoid social situations.</li><li>Experience decreased self-esteem.</li></ul>

What to do about bullying:

Do This:	Not this:
• Get the facts from multiple sides if possible. • Listen to the feelings, and add that you want to help. • Role-play possible responses. • Take it seriously. • Help them figure out how to avoid the places where bullying happens. • Suggest they stay around other kids or adults (bullies often target someone who is alone). • Consider ways to increase assertiveness. • Consider if it's better to avoid the bully altogether.	• Avoid blaming or labeling. • Don't fault the victim; it's already difficult to talk about the experience. • Don't encourage retaliation, because it could make it worse. • Don't immediately contact the other parent, because that could make it worse too.

What if your kid is the one bullying others? It doesn't mean you're a bad parent. It is a sign that your son or daughter needs some extra guidance. Take it seriously. Try to understand the reasons for the bullying, and address the needs. Is it about trying to fit in with a particular group? Is it about stress? Are they also being bullied? Also, involve your son or daughter in making amends.

Answer 2: Support after a suicide

Why I picked it:

After watching the episode, I noted the extent of blame from Hannah and the guilt feelings among her classmates. Since suicide is a major, recurring theme, I've broken it into three parts with this being the first (see also Answers 7 and 11).

Primary resource:

Suicide Awareness/Voices of Education (SAVE; **https://www.save.org/**) is one of the leading suicide prevention organizations in the world and is a leading champion of media guidelines around reporting on suicide. SAVE was founded by people who had experienced suicides of family members, and continues to have grief support as a core part of their mission. SAVE has put out "talking points" about 13RW as well as a webinar: **http://go.kognito.com/13reasonswhywebinar.html**.

Terminology:

- **Suicide attempt** means that someone does something to himself or herself with at least some intent to die (e.g., "He attempted suicide" or "She tried to kill herself").
- **Suicide attempt survivor** means someone who had a suicide attempt and did not die from it.
- **Suicide** is when a suicide attempt ends in death (e.g., "She died by suicide").
- **Suicide loss survivor** means someone who has lost a family member or friend to suicide.
- **Suicidal behavior** includes all suicide-related activity including planning, attempts, and death.

How common is suicide?

From the Centers for Disease Control and Injury Prevention (CDC) data for 2015:

- Suicide is the 10th leading cause of death in the United States with over 40,000 deaths by suicide each year.
- Suicide is the second leading cause of death for people ages 10 to 24 years old in the US (accidents are number one – see Answer 10).
- Overall, 13 out of 100,000 people die by suicide. The rate is higher for males (21 per 100,000) than it is for females (6 per 100,000).

Effects of suicide (on loss survivors):

From *Responding to Grief, Trauma, and Distress After a Suicide: U.S. National Guidelines* by the Survivors of Suicide Loss Task Force: "the experience of suicide loss survivors" may include:

- Questioning what caused the suicide, and how much the person wanted to die.
- Dealing with the stigma, shame, negativity, mystery, and silence that surround suicide.
- Trauma from the loss, having witnessed the death or imagining the death.
- Feeling shame, particularly as others question the moral standing and character of the person who died by suicide.
- Blaming others, or blaming themselves for the death, or feeling guilty about what they believe they might have been able to do if the person was still alive.
- Experiencing feelings of abandonment or rejection.
- Feelings of anger at themselves or others, including towards the person who died by suicide.
- A sense of relief is also sometimes present if the suicide ended a prolonged period of pain and struggle (e.g., when someone has constant battles with depression or substance abuse).

(http://actionallianceforsuicideprevention.org/task-force/survivors-suicide-loss)

SAVE also notes that if grief does not get processed, then it can cause relationship problems, ongoing distress, physical illness, depression, and increased suicide risk.

Understanding suicide:

SAVE answers these frequently asked questions:

Why do people kill themselves?

There are no simple answers. In addition to all the potential stress and negative experiences like those depicted in 13RW, an estimated 90% of people who die by suicide have struggled with a mental health problem like depression or a substance abuse issue. SAVE emphasizes that "with awareness, education, and treatment, people can be helped."

Are suicide attempts just ways to prove something or get sympathy?

It's a warning that something is incredibly wrong in someone's life and can be taken as a "cry for help." The suicidal person is reacting to significant pain and hopelessness. Every suicide attempt should be taken seriously because without a positive change there's a chance for another, possibly deadly, suicide attempt in the future.

Do you have a greater risk for suicide after knowing someone who dies by suicide?

There is a higher risk for multiple reasons. For one, some genes make suicidal behavior run in families. There is also the chance that someone with suicide risk based on other things might get prompted to engage in suicidal behavior following a suicide death.

Can you stop a suicide even after someone has made up their mind?
SAVE answers forcefully: "Absolutely! Never give up on someone contemplating suicide."

Your experience:

Do you know someone who died by suicide? If so, then first let me just say that I'm sorry someone in your life died this way. I know a lot of loss survivors and each story carries a pain that I feel deeply. Was it a family member? A friend? Did you get a chance to grieve? The resources from SAVE may be helpful whether your loss was recent, or if it was in the distant past. Do you have experience with feeling suicidal yourself? (Please refer to the discussion in Answer 7 as well).

If you have any personal experience with suicide, then you will probably have a range of feelings about the series (and the characters). You might react to things differently than someone who has no personal connection to the topic. It could be helpful for your son or daughter to know why. Also, while I know it's not a comforting thought, suicidal behavior has some genetic elements. Thus, if there is a family history of suicide then your son or daughter may have inherited some risk factors, and it's better for them to know rather than remain unaware. On the other side of the coin, they can also know that they have family who has learned to live with and overcome those risks.

Signs of grief:

- Many parts of grieving are normal or expected, for example:
    - Talking about the loss all the time; or not talking about it at all (e.g., extremes).
    - Crying, including at unexpected times.
    - Talking about "seeing" or "feeling" the presence of the person who died.
    - Being angry or irritable, or having trouble concentrating.
    - Wanting to be physically or emotionally closer to family or friends.

- You might be more concerned if:
    - Normal grieving seems on the extreme side or continues for a long time.
    - They start taking more dangerous risks.
    - They are withdrawing from people and activities.
    - Dramatic changes in personality or functioning happen for an extended time.
    - They start talking about wanting to die.

- If someone has recently experienced the suicide of a family member, friend, or peer, then he or she should get every possible opportunity to talk about it, and be encouraged to seek support.

What to do after a suicide:

1. Work through the immediate thoughts, questions, and emotions regarding the loss. Two factors that can influence the impact of suicide: (1) When did it happen (e.g., recent or distant)? (2) How close was the relationship (e.g., family, acquaintance)?

2. Process through the grief cycle. SAVE offers these tips:
   - It's okay to cry; it is a natural expression of deep sorrow.
   - It's okay to heal and not to feel guilty about it.
   - Laughing at happy memories is okay.
   - It could be useful to find support: family, friend, support groups (**https://www.save.org/save-support-groups/**).

3. Get help for the current distress. SAVE also offers wallet cards, booklets, and books via their web store (**https://www.save.org/find-help/coping-with-loss/**).

4. Your local crisis center can also help with identifying resources. In the US, you can call the National Suicide Prevention Lifeline (800-273-8255) to access the network 24/7.

5. As a follow-up, talk through the traits and experiences that your son or daughter has that might resemble the person who died by suicide (note that this could also apply to talking about the fictional suicide of Hannah in 13RW). Compare those traits and experiences to the suicide risk factors (Answer 7) and warning signs (Answer 11).

Answer 3: Mental health screening and treatment

Why I picked it:

This episode has teasing and sexual harassment, but as I watched I also had a growing concern about many of the teens' mental health and substance abuse. So, I decided to focus broadly on mental health and mental illness for this chapter.

Primary resource:

My primary recommendation is Mental Health America (MHA; **http://www.mentalhealthamerica.net/**), a community-based nonprofit that has focused on mental health promotion for more than 100 years. At around the same time that I was writing this book, they held a Facebook Live discussion about 13RW that has been viewed by over 10,000 people, earning them my top spot. (You can access the recorded conversation here if you wish: **https://www.mentalhealthamerica.net/tags/13-reasons-why**).

Terminology:

- **Mental health** is the ability to think clearly, be part of healthy social relationships, and feel positive emotions.
- **Mental health challenges** include anything that disrupts mental health, whether or not it qualifies as a diagnosable condition
- **Mental illness** is an identified pattern of symptoms the damages or interferes with mental health (also called psychiatric disorder, psychiatric diagnosis, mental disorder).
- **Substance abuse** involves using a chemical or drug in a way that disrupts mental health.
- **Substance dependence** is when alcohol or another drug(s) are used on a regular basis (e.g., daily or in binges), attempts to stop using are unsuccessful, or there is a physical or mental "need" for it (also called substance use disorder, or addiction).
- **Behavioral health** is a term used when mental health and substance abuse are considered together.

How common are mental health challenges in the US?

- More than 16 million adults have dealt with major depression.
- Over 42.5 million adults have dealt with severe anxiety.
- At least 14 million adults have suffered from increased anxiety following a traumatic event.
- Substance abuse directly affects more than 25 million adults (alcohol alone is approximately 10 million).

Effects of mental health challenges include:

- The direct negative impact of symptoms.
- Declining school performance.
- Withdrawing from friends or activities.
- Increased tension in relationships.
- Missing appointments due to forgetting, or low concentration.
- Sleep deficits due to insomnia.
- Increased risk for suicidal behavior.

Why talk about mental health? Sometimes the things that are interfering with mental health will just pass on their own (e.g., temporary stress). However, at times things need additional attention. There's no reason to suffer from physical, mental, emotional, or social distress. Effective treatment and support options are available.

Understanding mental health challenges:

Pretty much every behavioral health issue could be understood as a combination of biology and environment:
- Biology: Our DNA (genetics) sets up our biochemicals, brain functions, and elements of temperament or personality that can play a role in mental health. Later, everything from nerve activity to hormone responses contributes to how we think and feel.
- Environment: Past experiences create memories, response patterns, and changes in brain and body. Then, the mix of supports and stress, from the outside and inside, have an impact on what parts of our lives are more (or less) healthy. Note that significant stress including things like repeated bullying can trigger symptoms of a mental health condition.
- One form of anxiety that shows up in the teens following the suicide in 13RW is some degree of Post-Traumatic Stress Disorder (PTSD). According to MHA, PTSD can affect "anyone who was a victim,

witnessed or has been exposed to a life-threatening situation." Specific examples include domestic violence, rape, car accidents, child abuse, combat experience, or unexpected sudden death like suicide.

Sometimes, the answer to what can help address a mental health challenge is straightforward, but as you can imagine, at other times it can get complicated. That's why it might make sense to talk to a professional for help. In most cases, treatment can successfully address depression for example, but only a third of people experiencing severe depression seek professional help.

Your experience:

How's your mental health? Are there challenges you're dealing with right now? Consider completing a screening for yourself. MHA has free, online, instant screening assessments available for depression, anxiety, PTSD, alcohol and substance use, and other issues (**http://www.mentalhealthamerica.net/mental-health-screening-tools**). Think of it as setting a good example for your son or daughter. Taking care of yourself also helps you have the mental and emotional wellness to care for your family.

Were there any mental health challenges that you had in the past? Do you have a family history of mental health concerns? As noted earlier, many of the behavioral health issues have some genetic parts, so it can help your son or daughter to know what might "run in the family." It can also help him or her not feel alone if mental health concerns pop up, because they'll know someone who has dealt with them before. Also, please know that some of the same genes that increase the risk for some mental health challenges can have beneficial sides too, and you can help your son or daughter access those inherited strengths (see Answer 8 for one example). The National Alliance on Mental Illness (NAMI; **https://www.nami.org/**) is another excellent resource that has useful information for the family.

What if you're doing ok, but your kid needs help? Are you worried you won't be able to relate? It's okay. All behavioral health concerns, from minor stress through the worst mental illness symptoms, are just extremes of everyday experiences. Even if you have the same diagnosis as another person, there will be differences. Identify the primary concern, and think about what it resembles. Then, note that you don't have the same experience, but in some ways, it seems similar to something you do know. Mention what appears to be a match and ask how their experience differs. Use your experience as a way to establish common grounds for empathy, and as a starting point for conversation. For example, "I've never had hallucinations before, but it sounds like times when I had nightmares that seemed so real that I'd wake up sweating and my heart would be pounding. Are your hallucinations anything like that? In what ways are they different?"

Finally, if everything is fine all around (or later, after addressing concerns), check out MHA tips for further boosting your mental health: **http://www.mentalhealthamerica.net/31-tips-boost-your-mental-health**

Signs of mental health challenges:

As a parent, you can complete a brief screening report about your son or daughter to get a sense of what might be cause for concern. Your child can also complete a short youth screening that is designed for ages 10 to 17 years old. Both forms are available here: **http://www.mentalhealthamerica.net/mental-health-screening-tools**

Symptoms of depression	Symptoms of PTSD
• Sad, anxious, or empty mood	• Nightmares
• Sleep changes	• Flashbacks
• Loss of interest or pleasure	• Thoughts that come up all the time
• Irritability	• Easy to startle
• Fatigue and low energy	• Unable to concentrate
• Guiltiness	• Can't sleep
• Hopelessness	• Emotionally numb
• Worthlessness	• Detached from others
• Suicidal feelings	• Avoiding reminders of the trauma

What to do to help with mental health challenges:

See the MHA resources for talking to adolescents and teens with signs that you need to talk about mental health, starting the conversation, and what to do that are available on their website: (**http://www.mentalhealthamerica.net/conditions/talking-adolescents-and-teens-time-talk**). I'll provide a summary for you here:

- Choose a time and place that will be low stress and low pressure.
- Consider talking while doing a shared activity.
- You can start the conversation by talking about signs you've noticed that have made you curious or concerned.
- Know the three most common treatment forms and what's available to you:
    - Therapy is when a trained mental health professional helps someone explore thoughts, feelings, and actions with the goal of addressing problems and increasing wellness.
    - Medication includes a variety of drugs that have been developed to help manage symptoms, and companies are always creating better ones.
    - Support groups are meetings of multiple people where the goal is sharing social support and assisting each other's goals for recovery or wellness.

Do this:	Not this:
• Listen to their experience.	• Don't minimize or downplay their thoughts or feelings.
• Ask what they think might help.	
• Learn about the mental health concern ahead of time.	• Don't let your emotions (especially anger) take over.
• Tell them that mental health challenges are common, and people recover.	• Don't label things.
	• Avoid saying what they "should do."
• It's okay to admit your concern and fears.	• Avoid arguing about specifics.
• Offer possibilities for confidential help.	• Don't make excuses or blame other people or places.
• Be persistent about finding the right support or treatment match for your son or daughter.	• Avoid making comparisons to others (especially siblings).

Answer 4: Help for victims of crime

Why I picked it:

The episode centers on stalking, so that was my first selection. However, that seemed perhaps too narrow. I've thus expanded it to crime victimization more generally.

Primary resource:

The National Center for Victims of Crime (NCVC; **https://victimsofcrime.org/**) focuses on "victims' rights and helping victims of crime rebuild their lives." I found them after landing on the Stalking Resource Center website (**https://victimsofcrime.org/our-programs/stalking-resource-center**) and seeing that it was part of the larger organization.

Terminology:

- **Theft** is when someone takes your property while you're not there.
- **Vandalism** includes breaking or damaging property.
- **Property crime** is taking or destroying things, including theft and vandalism.
- **Assault** is a physical attack on a person.
- **Robbery** is when someone takes something from you directly.
- **Violent crime** includes assault, rape, robbery, and homicide.
- **Personal crime** is potentially violent crimes that are against a person directly.
- **Hate crime** is when any property or personal crime is motivated by bias against race, religion, disability, ethnicity, or sexual orientation.
- **Stalking** is a series of behaviors directed at a particular person in a way that generates fear.

How common are personal crimes?

- The rate of violent crime has decreased significantly since 1994 but has increased a little beginning in 2010.
- In the US, more than two-thirds of teens (ages 14 to 17 years old) have experienced assault at some point in their lives.
- Violent crimes at school peaked in 1993, and have declined since then, but it still occurs yearly in almost 3 out of 4 public schools.
- Each year in the United States, 7.5 million people experience stalking.
- Over their lifetimes, 15% of women and 6% of men will have had a stalker.
- Approximately 1 in 7 victims of stalking was between ages 11 and 17 years old.

Effects of crime on victims:

Typical reactions after being victimized by a crime include:

- Feeling angry, sad, or lonely.
- Not being able to sleep.
- Feeling guilty or ashamed.
- Feeling sick and having no appetite.
- Wanting to hurt someone.
- Feeling hopeless.
- Feeling afraid or anxious.
- Wanting to defend oneself.
- Feeling like there are no friends.
- Finding it hard to trust others.
- Difficulty concentrating in school, or at work.
- Feeling traumatized.

Understanding crime:

Males are disproportionately involved in crime, particularly violent crime, as both perpetrators and victims. Men predominately commit some crimes against women (e.g., stalking, sexual violence). By age, young people (ages 16–24 years old) experience the most crime both as victims and offenders.

Stalking

Stalking is considered a crime in all 50 US states and can be classified as a felony if it is recurrent or violent.

Most of the time, the stalker was someone known either as a romantic partner or as an acquaintance. Stalkers become obsessed with a particular person and can progress from basic information gathering to repeat contacts (e.g., notes, calls, requests for a date), to threats and vandalism, all the way up to murder or attempted murder. The Stalking Resource Center has facts, information, safety guides, and support.

Criminal Justice system

Law enforcement	Court system	Corrections
<ul><li>Takes crime reports</li><li>Investigates</li><li>Arrests offenders</li></ul>	<ul><li>Lawyers - Prosecution vs. Defense Attorney</li><li>Review evidence</li><li>Make a court case</li><li>Judge reviews case</li></ul>	<ul><li>Jail (short term)</li><li>Prison (long-term)</li><li>Parole</li><li>Probation</li></ul>

Your experience:

Have you ever been the victim of a crime? If so, then take the time to think about your experience as two parts: internal (your thoughts and feelings) and external (the crime itself, actions by you and others afterward). I suggest this because a lot may be different on the external parts of the crime experience, and it's easy to get caught up in the differences. What is most likely to be similar is the internal part. Stated another way, even when the specifics of your experience don't match, what you know about how it feels is key. When a new crime happens, advice you might offer based on your experience with the criminal justice system could be correct, but it might also be inaccurate or incomplete. Using what you know about the internal process is a safer bet. Victim assistance resources can help with figuring out the external procedures.

There are lessons in times when you've avoided being victimized by crime as well. More than likely, there are things that you do on a regular basis to protect yourself and your property that might even be automatic now (i.e., safety habits). That is particularly likely if you've ever lived in an area with high crime. Take some time to think about the steps you take so that you can pass on those specific tips to your son or daughter (or others). We can help our next generation avoid needing to "learn the hard way."

Signs of being victimized by crime include:

- A sudden change in behavior.
- Acting more aggressive or provocative.
- Seeking attention, being "clingy."
- Risk-taking behavior.
- Expressions of being powerless or helpless.
- Fear of going to school.

What to do after a crime:

Do you know of a crime that has happened? Did someone do something to your son or daughter, or one of their friends? Stay calm and focus on your teen's needs. Avoid judging and just listen. Try to balance between accepting their emotions and setting limits (e.g., not allowing violent reactions). Help your teen feel in control of the response by providing options. Potential options include reporting it to the police or school, accessing mental health resources, and contacting victim services.

Say this:	Not this:
• Nothing you did or didn't do made you deserve it.	• This wouldn't have happened if you just...
• I'm glad you told me.	• This is all my fault.
• How can we help you feel safe?	• I told you not to...
• I'll support your decisions.	• Get over it.
• I'm sorry this happened.	• Just forget about it.
• I believe you.	• I want to kill the person who did it.

If someone has victimized your teen, then you can help them to process through the anxiety, grief, trauma, and other reactions. Dealing successfully with the negative emotions and learning coping methods can help them grow their resiliency. A useful resource may be the Victim Connect Resource Center (855-4-VICTIM).

Answer 5: Support for LGBTQ youth

Why I picked it:

Decisions about "coming out" as LGBTQ are the dominant theme of the episode, accompanied by one character having gay dads and discussing her experience growing up as their daughter.

Primary resource:

The Trevor Project (**http://www.thetrevorproject.org/**) has been helping LGBTQ youth work through issues and resolve crises for nearly 20 years. I'll mention some other resources here as well, but honestly, Trevor Project is my recommendation because (a) they do great work, and (b) I know and trust their staff.

Terminology:

- **LGBTQ** stands for Lesbian, Gay, Bisexual, Trans(gender), Questioning (or Queer).
- **Sexual orientation** means who you are physically attracted.
- **Gender identity** is your tendency or feeling about gender role.
- **Lesbian** means a woman mainly attracted to other women.
- **Gay** means a man primarily attracted to other men, but is also used more generally for same-sex attractions.
- **Bisexual** means that someone is attracted to both males and females.
- **Trans** means someone whose gender identity is different from the gender assigned at birth.
- **Questioning** implies that a person is exploring or questioning their sexual orientation or gender identity.

How many people identify as LGBTQ?

According to a 2012 Gallup survey of more than 100,000 US adults:

- 3.4% identified themselves as lesbian, gay, bisexual, or transgender.
- An additional 4.4% selected "don't know" or declined to answer the question. This group may include individuals who have some degree of attraction to the same sex but do not identify as primarily LGBT.
- Young adults (ages 18 to 25 years old) were far more likely than older adults (over 65 years old) to identify as LGBT (6.4% versus 1.9%).

Effects of stigma and social stress on LGBTQ youth:

LGBTQ youth are more likely than their peers to experience:
- Suicidal behavior
- Bullying
- Substance abuse
- Depression
- Anxiety
- Risky sexual behaviors (including sexual assault)

The family and social environment are critical parts of this pattern that can be changed to be more accepting and supportive.

Understanding sexual orientation and gender identity:

In 2014, the American Psychological Association and National Association of School Psychologists adopted a Resolution on Gender and Sexual Orientation Diversity in Children and Adolescents (**http://www.apa.org/about/policy/orientation-diversity.aspx**). It states in part:

> *"people express and experience great diversity in sexual orientation and gender identity and expression... some children and adolescents are aware of their attraction to members of the same gender or of their status as lesbian, gay, or bisexual persons by early adolescence... some children and adolescents may experience a long period of questioning their sexual orientations or gender identities, experiencing stress, confusion, fluidity or complexity in their feelings and social identities...*

THEREFORE BE IT RESOLVED that the American Psychological Association and the National Association of School Psychologists affirm that same-sex sexual and romantic attractions, feelings, and behaviors are normal and positive variations of human sexuality regardless of sexual orientation identity;

BE IT FURTHER RESOLVED that the American Psychological Association and the National Association of School Psychologists affirm that diverse gender expressions, regardless of gender identity, and diverse gender identities, beyond a binary classification, are normal and positive variations of the human experience;"

Acceptance of gay and lesbian relationships has increased over time. According to a Gallup report, in 2002 only 38% of US adults considered gay and lesbian relationships to be "morally acceptable," but that number increased to 54% by 2012. In 1977, 56% of US adults thought that being gay or lesbian was a result of upbringing and environment, and only 13% said it was a trait present at birth. As of 2012, 40% say sexual orientation is a birth characteristic, and 35% say it is the result of environment.

Your experience:

Do you identify as LGBTQ? Think about your journey in arriving at your sexual and gender identity. It's useful to talk about the challenges you faced, what may have changed since you first "came out," and any concerns you might have as an LGBTQ parent (e.g., about how others see you or treat you, or how they interact with your son or daughter). However, also think about the positive aspects of your experience in actively deciding to pursue your identity, discovering who you are attracted to and how you feel, and perhaps in finding your community. Those are types of positive experiences that can assist your teen regardless of his or her orientation and identity. A potential resource is Gay Parent Magazine (**http://www.gayparentmag.com/**).

What if your teen doesn't know about your sexual orientation or gender identity? There are many possible reasons for having parts of identity that you hide from your son or daughter. I'm not going to judge, but they might, so it would be a good idea to explore your reasons and make a conscious decision about what to share or withhold. Consider this resource:

The group Children of Lesbians and Gays Everywhere (COLAGE; **https://www.colage.org/**) has advice and resources for coming out to your kids or ongoing discussions about your sexual orientation and identity. They suggest finding a calm, comfortable, private place for a potentially long conversation. Prep yourself ahead of time because the possible responses vary widely. COLAGE has tips, stories from children, and resource recommendations.

What can you bring from your experience if you identify as heterosexual? Think about the people you've considered attractive over the years. Even if they were all of the opposite genders, there are probably multiple ways that they differed from each other in appearance or characteristics. How did you know who you found attractive? How did it feel inside? Were you nervous about telling others about your attraction? Did you ever feel like other people were judging who you decided to date? How different did it feel when people were happy about who you were dating? These are just some of the questions that could relate to universal experiences in social and intimate relationships. Regardless of differences in orientation or identity, we want to be loved, accepted, supported and encouraged. Find common ground in your experience of learning to balance between your natural attractions and the social or cultural expectations of others, then offer what you would have wanted to receive.

Signs of being LGBTQ?

Rather than trying to guess about sexual orientation or gender identity, I'm going to pass along these tips from the site **MyKidisGay.com** which also has resources for discussion of topics like religion and faith, sex, gender identity, and bullying.

- Support their overall experience of growing into themselves, whoever that will be.
- Don't make assumptions about orientation, just help them feel safe and supported for any orientation.
- Let them know you love and support them no matter what.
- Don't pressure your son or daughter to choose, and disclose a sexual orientation.

What you can do:

Please know that how you react to your teen's emerging sexual and gender identity has an enormous impact on them. If they experience rejection or unfavorable judgment at home, then they are more likely to have poor health outcomes. However, LGBTQ teens who feel valued and supported by their parents are significantly less likely to experience depression, turn to alcohol and drugs, engage in the risky sexual behavior, or become suicidal.

Recommended steps:
- Have an open discussion about sexual orientation and gender identity.
- Talk about school experiences including potential positive supports, and also painful experiences such as teasing or bullying.
- Understand that talking about sex and sexuality can be embarrassing, anxiety-provoking, or stressful.
- Be calm, respectful, and willing to listen.

The Trevor Project has a program called "Coming out As You." Their program includes a printable card that has identity dimensions that would be useful for discussion (biological sex, gender identity, gender expression, gender presentation, and sexual orientation). There is also a worksheet to help your teen organize his or her thoughts about the process of exploring this topic and "coming out."

If your son or daughter, or someone they know, is struggling with these issues and in crisis or suicidal, the Trevor Project has support specifically developed for LGBTQ teens and young adults (**http://www.thetrevorproject.org/pages/get-help-now**):

- Trevor Lifeline: 866-488-7386. Available 24/7
- Trevor chat (online instant messaging)
- Trevor text (text "Trevor" to 202-304-1200.
- TrevorSpace (online peer to peer community)

You can help your school as well.

Trevor Project has a free training resource specific for educators, school counselors, and school nurses called the Lifeguard Workshop (**http://www.thetrevorproject.org/pages/lifeguard**). The workshop is designed to help professionals identify key challenges related to LGBTQ issues, recognize warning signs of suicide risk, and respond to crisis situations.

Answer 6: Substance abuse prevention and treatment

Why I picked it:

At this point in 13RW, it might seem like all teens are drinking alcohol, or perhaps doing other drugs, and thus it made sense to do a reality check on that idea.

Primary resource:

For more than 30 years the Partnership for Drug-Free Kids (**http://drugfree.org/**) has been supporting families and communities to address drinking and drug problems. They started with anti-drug advertising and have grown from there. I worked with an affiliate group in Arizona while doing an evaluation of substance abuse prevention services and they excelled. I've held the group in high esteem ever since.

Terminology & How common are teen drug problems?

One of the best information resources is the Parents' Drug Guide that is available through The Partnership for Drug-Free Kids (**http://drugfree.org/drug-guide/**). Here is some of the information about common drugs and signs of long-term use or abuse:

Drug	Street names	How common?	Signs of abuse
Alcohol	Booze, 8-ball, brew	Past year: 50%	Slowed speech, nausea, vomiting, loss of coordination
Marijuana	blunt, boom, dope, grass, hash, herb, Mary Jane, pot, reefer, skunk, weed	Lifetime: 50%	slower thinking, lack of coordination, paranoia
Tobacco and cigarettes	cancer sticks, chew, dip, fags, smokes	Past month: 20%	causes yellowing of fingers and teeth, the smell lingers in hair and clothes
Inhalants such as paint thinners and glues	bagging, huffing, poppers, snappers, dusting, whippets	Lifetime: 1 out of 6	drunk, dazed, or dizzy feelings

Drug	Street names	How common?	Signs of abuse
Cough medicine	Dex, red devils, robo, triple C, tussin, skittles, syrup	Lifetime: 1 out of 7	loss of coordination, slurred or drunk speech, vomiting
Ecstasy	Adam, bean, E, roll, X, XTC	Lifetime: 1 out of 8	chills, teeth clenching, sweats, dehydration, anxiety
Prescription stimulants	Ritalin, Adderall, Dexedrine	Lifetime: 1 out of 8	high energy, minimal appetite, high alertness
Cocaine or crack	Big C, blow, bump, coke, nose candy, rock, snow	Lifetime: 1 out of 10	slurred speech, loss of coordination, nausea, vomiting

Effects of alcohol and substance abuse include:

- Substance dependence / addiction.
- Substance-related legal problems (e.g., arrest for illegal possession, DUI).
- Liver damage.
- Death of brain cells.
- Difficulty with school or work.
- Increased anxiety or depression.
- Increased risk of accidental injury.

Understanding alcohol and substance abuse:

Alcohol abuse

The average age of first alcohol use in the US is 14 years old, and 40% of teens think there's nothing wrong with having one to two drinks almost every day. Nearly 90% of teen drinking involves binge drinking (e.g., party drinking). Especially given the poor impulse control of the adolescent brain, the surge of alcohol with binge drinking makes risky behavior skyrocket. Additionally, problems with alcohol use as a teen set up a much higher chance for alcohol abuse later in life.

Risk factors for substance abuse include:

- A family history of substance abuse.
- Mental health issues such as depression, anxiety, or ADHD.
- History of trauma.
- Impulsive tendencies.

Reasons teens give for substance use include:

- Seeing parents, other adults, and peers drinking or smoking.
- Seeing it as normal based on TV and movies.
- Using it as a temporary escape from unhappiness.
- Using it as a relief from being lonely or bored.
- Rebelling against someone or something.
- Seeking immediate benefits.
- Attempting to overcome self-doubt or lack of confidence.

Your experience:

How much alcohol do you drink? Do you ever drink a little too much? Way too much? Have you ever in the past? How much do you smoke? Have you ever tried other drugs?

Be prepared for your son or daughter to ask about your experiences with alcohol and drugs. Be honest, but don't feel compelled to share every detail. Remember that your focus is on their realistic understanding of the topic so that they can make healthy decisions. Stay calm, ask them questions as you describe things, and your honesty can set the stage for their open communication as well.

Do you need to take care of your own substance use? You can set a good example for your teen, and his or her friends, by getting help for yourself first.

If you've ever used alcohol, tobacco, or another drug, then you can identify with reasons why your son or daughter might be interested in having a drink or smoke. Unlike your teen, you likely have experience with a variety of ways to achieve certain goals (e.g., relaxing, coping with anxiety). You can empathize with what your son or daughter is feeling, and help walk through the potential ways for them to meet their needs, including an honest discussion of possible benefits and consequences. You are helping them learn about decision-making so that they can make informed and (hopefully) healthy choices.

Signs of alcohol or substance abuse include:

- Using gum or mints to cover the smell.
- Frequent use of eye drops or nasal sprays.
- Frequently breaking curfew.
- Sudden appetite changes.
- Slurred speech, clumsy actions, or loss of coordination.
- Significant mood changes.
- Agitation or irritability.
- Flushed or red facial appearance.
- Missing class or school activities.
- Frequent headaches.
- Dry mouth, or being extra thirsty.
- Sores or spots near the mouth.
- Frequent nosebleeds.
- Increased accidents.
- Sweating a lot.

The Partnership for Drug-Free Kids has a complete list of warning signs available. It can also be useful to check out the page "Prevention tips for every age" which include scripts for discussion topics like if your teen comes home smelling like alcohol or cigarettes for the first time, or they start hanging out with a new group of kids you don't know (**http://drugfree.org/article/prevention-tips-for-every-age/**).

Most relevant to the 13RW topic is a discussion after watching a movie or show that has drug use:

"I'm sorry if this seems overprotective but that show bothered me, and now I'm curious about your experience. Do your friends dabble with drugs? Do they drink often? How do you feel about it?"

What you can do:

To prevent alcohol and substance abuse:

> ### What are social host laws?
>
> Depending on your state laws, adults that host a party providing alcohol to minors can face fines and even prison time. They may also be held liable if an accident occurs involving a minor who is drinking alcohol at their party.

- Restrict teen access to your alcohol.
- Supervise teen parties.
- Clearly communicate your expectations for their party or social time (e.g., regular check-ins).
- Tell them you, or someone you trust can pick them up whenever needed.
- Establish regular communication with open discussion of issues.
- Listen without judging (as much as possible) when your kid says he or she is interested in drinking or drugs.
- Offer empathy, compassion, and understanding.
- Reassure your son or daughter that you want to provide love and support, but also guidance for his or her long-term health and safety.

To help when substance abuse is an issue:

If your son or daughter, or one of their friends, is abusing alcohol or drugs then you may need to have an "intervention" conversation. You can download an "Intervention e-book" with detailed guidance (**http://drugfree.org/download/intervention-ebook/**), but the basic idea is to:

- Have a clear plan.
- Pick a calm and sober time to talk.
- Be objective about the warning signs you see.
- Let them know why you care.
- Ask open questions and actively listen.
- To whatever degree that you can, make it "a conversation rather than a confrontation."

The partnership also has a "marijuana talk kit" focused on specific questions, concerns, and tips for that issue as well (**http://drugfree.org/download/marijuana-talk-kit/**).

Treatment options:

Treatment types range from outpatient counseling at a specialty site up through residential or inpatient programs lasting more than a month depending on a person's needs. There will usually be some combination of treatments possibly including individual counseling, support groups, educational sessions, life skills lessons, family engagement, and treatment of mental health concerns.

Check out the "treatment e-book" (**http://drugfree.org/download/treatment-ebook/**) as well as the website sections on navigating the treatment system (**http://drugfree.org/article/navigating-the-treatment-system/**).

The Partnership for Drug Free Kids also has sources for support from fellow parents including a parent blog, and parent coaches (**http://drugfree.org/landing-page/get-help-support/support-from-other-parents/**).

There's even a helpline available on weekdays 9 am to 5 pm Eastern with trained counselors who can assist (855-DRUGFRE), or online chat weekdays 5 pm to 10 pm Eastern, and 12 pm to 5 pm Eastern on weekends.

Note: You can also locate treatment through this website: **http://findtreatment.samhsa.gov**.

Answer 7: Counter suicide risk, enhance protection

Why I picked it:

This episode shows some suicide prevention messaging happening at the school, and some missed opportunities when someone could have helped Hannah. Thus, it is an appropriate episode to revisit suicidal risk.

Primary resource:

As of this year (2017), the American Foundation for Suicide Prevention (AFSP) has been sponsoring suicide prevention education and research for 30 years. Along with SAVE, AFSP has also been at the forefront of suicide prevention community response to 13RW. In collaboration with the National Association of School Psychologists and the American School Counselor Association (see Answer 13) they put together a webinar which you can access here if you wish: **https://afsp.org/teachable-moment-using-13-reasons-initiate-helpful-conversation-suicide-prevention-mental-health/**

Terminology:

- **Risk factor** means a characteristic or condition that increases the chance of suicide.
- **Protective factor** means a characteristic or condition that decreases the likelihood of suicide.

How common is suicidal risk in high school students?

The 2015 Youth Risk Behavior Survey asked students about their suicidal experiences in the past year and found that:

- 17.7% seriously considered suicide.
- 14.6% made a suicide plan.
- 8.6% made a suicide attempt.
- 2.8% made a suicide attempt that required treatment.

(https://www.cdc.gov/healthyyouth/data/yrbs/results.htm)

Effects of suicide attempts include:

- The risk of injury or death from suicidal behavior.
- Trauma for self and others.

Understanding suicidal behavior

Risk factors for suicidal behavior include:

- Suicidal history (prior suicide attempts, or family history of suicide).
- Mental illness (especially depression, bipolar disorder, schizophrenia, borderline personality disorder, anxiety disorder).
- Substance abuse issues.
- Negative and stressful life events like legal trouble, losing a job, divorce, or death of a family member or a close friend.
- Long-term (cumulative) stress from unemployment, problems with close relationships, bullying.
- Access to a lethal method like a gun or high dosage of medicine.
- Social isolation or withdrawal.

Protective factors (via Suicide Prevention Resource Center; **http://sprc.org**) include:

- Effective mental health or substance abuse treatment.
- Reliable social and community connections.
- Life skills for coping and problem-solving.
- A sense of meaning and purpose.
- Cultural, religious, or other beliefs that discourage suicide.

In 2012 the National Action Alliance for Suicide Prevention published the *National Strategy for Suicide Prevention* following a process that pulled from expertise across federal government agencies, suicide researchers, attempt and loss survivors, and leaders of suicide prevention organizations. It's available for free online: **http://actionallianceforsuicideprevention.org/national-strategy-suicide-prevention-0**

Suicide prevention strategies include:

- Finding people at risk and referring them to help or support.
- Providing education and encouraging help-seeking.
- Improving mental health and substance abuse services, and increasing access.
- Making it easier to transition from one service or support setting to another.
- Responding when someone is in crisis in helpful ways.
- Reducing access to the lethal methods of suicide (primarily guns and medicines).
- Enhancing life skills and fostering resilience.
- Promoting social connections and supports.
- Immediate and long-term support for those impacted by suicide.

Your experience:

Do you have any of the risk factors? What protective factors do you have? Some of those factors are historical, and can't be changed, but can be recognized (e.g., history of suicide attempt). It can be tempting to ignore or downplay our risk for something like suicide. Unfortunately, life sometimes dumps multiple sources of stress on people "all at once" or "like dominoes," and it's much harder to counter risk during a crisis. Therefore, take the time to take care of any risk factors before life stress hits, and you'll be better off. Also, think about what protective factors you can strengthen or add to enhance your resilience. Remember, you have the potential to be one of your teen's top protective factors.

Don't forget to give yourself some credit too. You've made it past many years of life challenges and stress. What secrets and tips for coping, or problem-solving your way past risk factors could you pass on to your son or daughter?

Signs of suicide risk:

Could this information apply to your son or daughter? Compare the risk and protective factors listed above to your son or daughter's case. If there is a risk for your child, then as with your process, the trick is to address risk factors as early as possible and build up protection as well. Answer 11 discusses specific warning signs for immediate risk. However, if you have immediate concerns call the National Suicide Prevention Lifeline 24/7, and a trained counselor can assist: 800-273-TALK (8255).

What you can do:

Further developing your relationship with your son or daughter can strengthen the protection from social connections for them as well. Working through the topics in this book can help with improving the life skills that foster resilience. Someone can also counter suicide risk by getting effective treatment as early as possible.

There are also some specific treatments that help to decrease suicide risk. There are two types of therapy specifically developed for suicidal issues that have proven useful: Cognitive Behavioral Therapy for Suicide Prevention, and Dialectical Behavioral Therapy (DBT). Some medications may also help lower risk of suicidal behavior (e.g., clozapine, lithium, ketamine). Finally, effective treatment for conditions associated with suicide can help as well (e.g., depression, bipolar disorder, alcohol or substance abuse treatment).

AFSP funds research that tries to (a) understand suicidal behavior, (b) prevent suicidal behavior from occurring, (c) treat suicidal thoughts and feelings, and (d) respond in the aftermath of suicide. (See: (**https://afsp.org/our-work/research/research-grants/**)

They also have an outreach program offering peer support after a suicide and lists of support groups (**https://afsp.org/find-support/ive-lost-someone/**).

What can schools do?

AFSP, in partnership with the Trevor Project, the National Association of School Psychologists, and the American School Counselor Association, developed a *Model School Policy on Suicide Prevention* to provide guidance on comprehensive school-based suicide prevention (**https://afsp.org/our-work/education/model-school-policy-suicide-prevention/**).

Answer 8: Creative approaches to therapy

Why I picked it:

This episode focuses on Hannah's poetry experience, which presents the opportunity for talking about creative arts therapies.

Primary resource:

The National Coalition of Creative Arts Therapies Associations (NCCATA; **http://www.nccata.org/**) is an umbrella group for the professional associations that support creative arts therapies in the US. Through their website, you can get to any of the other groups (so I'm kind of able to cheat on this).

Terminology:

- **Creative arts therapies** use the creative arts (visual art, music, dance, drama, poetry) to help people understand, heal, and grow.
- The sections below include additional specific terms.

How common are creative arts therapies?

- The American Art Therapy Association has 5,000 members.
- The American Music Therapy Association says there are approximately 5,000 board-certified music therapists in the US.

Effects of mental health on art:

In her 1993 book, *Touched with Fire,* Kay Jamison explored the connections between artistic temperament and various types of mood disorders (e.g., depression and bipolar disorder). A link between creative arts and mental health challenges has been suspected for centuries, studied in a variety of ways, and remains controversial. Jamison's book stands apart as a beautifully written text on the subject. The primary connection to 13RW is to acknowledge that severe pain and personal expressions of distress can be manifest through creative arts (as with at least two characters in the show). On the one hand, this means that in addition to appreciating the teen artistry, you should also be aware of possible communication of trouble and despair that may need follow-up. On the other hand, it also shows how people can transform personal struggles in healthy ways through the arts.

Understanding creative arts therapies

There are trained professionals who purposely use the power of creative expression through the arts to help people communicate their inner experience. Thus, as an aside, if your son or daughter has an interest in arts, and you wonder if there is an actual job that might fit that interest, consider exploring these professional career paths.

Art therapists work with clients to develop, interpret, and discuss visual arts. They help people with problem-solving, conflict resolution, self-control, interpersonal relationships, stress reduction, and enhanced self-awareness. Because the initial focal point is nonverbal communication, it is sometimes possible for art therapy to work in cases where traditional talk therapy models are less useful.

There is existing research on the effectiveness of art therapy within several areas that could match many of the topics coming up in 13RW. A systematic review of research found that art therapy programs have:

- Decreased trauma symptoms among children and teens with a history of sexual abuse.
- Decreased symptoms of anxiety and PTSD for girls ages 8 to 17 years old with a history of sexual abuse.
- Improved mood and behavior with adult men in prison.
- Improved self-image and therapy engagement for depressed mothers.
- Decreased symptoms of depression and fatigue in adult cancer patients.
- Improved multiple dimensions of self-esteem for teen girls in a juvenile justice setting.

The American Art Therapy Association can help you find a qualified art therapist (**https://arttherapy.org/**).

Dance and movement therapists guide people through personal expression and use principles of mind-body connections to link movement to mental and emotional health. Many therapists focus on self-esteem and body image. A particular subject for dance therapy is helping women to recover from violence, assault, or trauma. The specific attention to integrating body and mind can help with the healing process. Some people struggling with eating disorders or PTSD may find this therapeutic approach beneficial for similar reasons as they seek to reconnect with their bodies in healthier ways. The American Dance Therapy Association can help you locate a trained dance or movement therapist (**https://adta.org/**).

In music therapy, the therapist works with someone through listening to particular music, creating music, or playing/singing music. The therapist uses music principles in assessment, and then through treatment specifically designed to achieve changes in mental and emotional health. Research has documented effectiveness at addressing symptoms of anxiety, stress, anger, aggression, physical pain, and even some parts of psychosis. Music therapy can often be incorporated successfully into school IEP plans as well.

The American Music Therapy Association can help you find a music therapist (**https://www.musictherapy.org/**).

Two additional approaches that are specialties that a clinician or therapist might use:

Drama therapy uses narratives, storytelling, and performance to change behaviors and improve relationships. Participants engage in role-plays, stories, and theater-based techniques in an active and experiential therapy. There is evidence for effectiveness in reducing some anxiety symptoms and increasing social skills. The North American Drama Therapy Association could help locate a program (**http://www.nadta.org/**).

Finally, the National Association for Poetry Therapy (**http://poetrytherapy.org/**) supports the use of **poetry** as part of therapeutic practice. It is considered a creative writing subdivision of bibliotherapy which uses written works within the context of therapy. The goal is to use creative writing to help promote healing and growth.

Your experience:

Do you have any experience with using art, music, dance, poetry, or some other creative outlet? If so, then consider sharing some of your work with your son or daughter. Perhaps you've noticed that you communicate better about some things using a different medium for expression than just sitting and talking. That might be useful either for your processing as you work through tough topics (like ones in this book) or helping reach out to your son or daughter. Whether you feel "artistic" or not, you might consider whether your teen might have an easier time talking through some things while working on some project with you.

Warning signs in creative work:

Does your child's art contain 'dark themes' like expressions of death, pain, injury, rage, sorrow, or loneliness? Especially take notice when such themes appear new, representing a change from their prior work. As noted in other chapters such shifts could be warning signs.

What to do:

Don't just let it go and assume it will pass. Ask about it. Where are they getting the motivation or experience? Is your son or daughter trying to communicate something to others?
If your teen seems to prefer expression through creative arts, perhaps try one of the creative arts therapies. It could be a worthwhile investment.

Answer 9: Awareness and prevention of sexual violence

Why I picked it:

This entire episode revolves around sexual assault after a girl gets drunk at a party. **There is a graphic depiction of the incident**. In researching that topic, many other related issues came up under the heading of sexual violence.

Primary resource:

Since 2000, The National Sexual Violence Resource Center (NSVRC; **http://www.nsvrc.org/**) has functioned as a "national information and resource hub relating to all aspects of sexual violence. They have an extensive collection and link to nearly every related organization in a well-organized directory.

Terminology:

- **Sexual violence** is perhaps the broadest term, including unwanted sexual contact by words or actions, from harassment through rape. It is forcing or manipulating someone into sexual activity without consent.
- **Sexual harassment** is unwelcome sexual statements, dating pressure, or intimate physical contact.
- **Sexual assault** is a broad term including any sexual activity without consent.
- **Drug-facilitated sexual assault** means a sexual assault that occurred after someone was under the influence of drugs (or alcohol) and unable to consent.
- **Dating violence** is physical, sexual, or emotional abuse within a dating relationship (related terms are date rape, intimate partner sexual assault, domestic violence, or intimate partner violence).

How common is sexual violence?

- Approximately 1 in 5 women and 1 in 71 men experience a rape incident at some point in their lives. More than half occur before the victim is 18 years old.
- In 8 out of 10 cases of sexual assault, the victim knew the perpetrator.
- 4 out of 5 parents don't know that teen dating violence is an issue.
- Approximately 1.5 million US high school students report having experienced some physical abuse from someone they were dating in the past year.
- Nearly 33% of teens in the US have experienced some form of abuse (physical, sexual, verbal) from someone they were dating. Approximately two out of five college women who are dating experience some dating violence.
- 1 in 6 women in college has been sexually abused while dating.

Effects of sexual violence:

A harmful or unhealthy dating relationship can have damaging impacts on teen development:

Immediate effects	Short-term impact	Long-term outcomes
• Fear • Confusion • Guilt • Loss of identity	• Poor school performance • Fighting • Binge drinking	• Substance abuse • Eating disorders • Suicidal behavior

Understanding sexual violence:

13RW does a great job at conveying that what qualifies as sexual harassment is based on how it feels to the victim regardless of the other person's intentions (e.g., joking, teasing, flirting). As in the show, sexual harassment can be the bridge between bullying and sexual assault, with a person sometimes escalating behavior from one category into another. There's also significant overlap between harassment and stalking (which Answer 4 covers). It is important to note that while stalking, harassment, and sexual assault are more likely to happen to women, both genders can be targets.

Regarding drug-facilitated sexual assault, most people would think of drugs that are often used for that purpose like GHB, Rohypnol (roofies), ketamine (Special K), meth, or ecstasy. However, it's important to know that the drug most frequently involved in sexual assault is alcohol.

Your experience:

Do you have personal experience with sexual violence? If so, then first let me say that I'm sorry that happened to you. You deserve to enjoy a respectful and healthy relationship, and I hope you have that now.

While the focus of this book is on teens, I also want to acknowledge that even if something happened to you in the distant past, these types of experiences could have lasting traumatic effects. Please take care of yourself too. There is absolutely no need to sit through the graphic depiction of assault if it might trigger traumatic memories for you. You don't have to prove you can "handle it." As with the topic of substance use, honest discussion about your personal knowledge of the issues can help your teen but don't feel like you need to talk about every detail.

Did you tell anyone about your experience before? Do you remember what that process was like when you were telling someone what happened for the first time? For people you've talked to, what did they do that was helpful or comforting? What would you want to improve about their response? Use those elements of your experience to help guide your approach with this discussion in case something does come to light. Also, think about any positive changes you may have made in your life after your experience (e.g., assertiveness, self-esteem, etc.). Those can be passed on to your son or daughter as prevention and mental health promotion.

Note: If you, or another adult, is currently in an ongoing relationship with someone that involves violence you can call The National Domestic Violence Hotline (NDVH) to speak with a trained advocate 24/7 at 800-799-7233; online chat available from 8 am to 3 am Eastern. If the person in an abusive relationship is a teen or young adult, then they can find a trained peer advocate through the NDVH project **LoveIsRespect.org** available 24/7 at 866-331-9474; online chat may also be available as well as texting support by sending the message "loveis" to 22522.

Signs of sexual violence include:

- Anxiety or fear of places or situations once considered safe.
- Failing grades or withdrawing from activities.
- An increase in alcohol or substance abuse.
- Having a partner who is controlling or dominating.
- Talk of a partner pressuring them into something unwanted.

What to do:

Does your son or daughter have experience with sexual violence? Does he or she know someone who does?

While it will probably be extremely challenging not to show shock or rage, your kid will need you to be calm and listen. Remember that there is no one "right way" for him or her to respond to the experience. Assure him or her of your love, and your willingness to support the recovery process. Let your teen know that you don't blame them for what happened. It's not the fault of the victim.

If dating violence has happened, and it is in the immediate aftermath, then it is highly recommended to get checked at a hospital or clinic. Even if there is no perceived injury, they can assess for subtle internal injuries and exposure to sexually transmitted infections. They are also trained in what evidence might be useful to collect, document, or save if someone plans to press charges. Also, if someone used a date rape drug, then a urine sample would be required to find out.

Given that the experience may come to light within the context of talking about 13RW, it's unlikely to be in the immediate past. In that case, the primary goals will be ensuring safety from that point forward (e.g., ending an abusive relationship, changing party habits, or peer group), coping with the emotional trauma, and determining whether to report an event to legal or other authorities. The counselors on the National Sexual Assault Hotline can help (800-656-HOPE). It is a confidential resource available 24/7.

How to deal with sexual harassment:

- The first thing to try, directly asking a person to stop, may sound obvious, but sometimes it is enough to work.
- If your son or daughter needs to ask another time, then tell the harasser that they will report the behavior if it continues.
- Your son or daughter (or friend) should confide in a trusted adult and ask for help.
- If things continue, and formal action is needed, then it will be helpful to make notes about what the person said or did including the date, time, location, and who witnessed it. Then, your son or daughter (or friend) should work with adult supports to report the harassment to the appropriate office or agency.

Answer 10: Promote safe driving

Why I picked it:

This episode centers on two related car accidents, and one is fatal. The series also shows multiple occasions where teens question whether someone is safe driving, or engage in reckless driving.

Primary resource:

The organization Students Against Destructive Decisions (SADD; http://www.sadd.org/) was originally named Students Against Driving Drunk, patterned after the group MADD (Mothers Against Drunk Driving). The name change for SADD reflected an expanded focus which, combined with a teen engagement emphasis, makes them my recommendation. For example, the group seeks to prevent teen substance abuse recognizing the significant impacts of alcohol and other drugs even when someone isn't driving. They have also developed efforts to promote personal health and safety including attention to suicide prevention.

Terminology:

- **Impaired driving** is when someone is operating a vehicle while affected by alcohol, drugs, illness, sleep deprivation, or other problems.
- **Drunk driving** is operating a vehicle while impaired by alcohol.
- **DUI** is a legal standard that stands for Driving Under the Influence and specifically applies to alcohol or drugs (also called DWI: Driving While Intoxicated).

How common are accidents due to impaired driving?

- Vehicle crashes are the leading cause of death for teens in the US.
- In 2015, over 2,700 teens (13 to 19 years old) died in motor vehicle accidents (CDC, WISQARS).
- As reported by SADD, more than 1 million injuries and 16,000 deaths in the US each year could be traced to impaired driving.

Effects of impaired driving include:

- Potential injury or death in an accident.
- Destruction or damage of property.
- Legal trouble or arrest.

Understanding impaired driving:

The crash fatality rates linked to alcohol are almost twice as high for teen drivers compared to adults. Younger drivers have a higher risk for accidents than adults even with less alcohol in their system. Recall from the substance abuse topic what effects drugs have, and their contribution to accidents is clear. Alcohol and drug abuse cause:

- Slower reaction time and reduce coordination.
- Difficulties with depth perception and peripheral vision.
- Hyperactivity or jitteriness from a high.
- Confusion or drowsiness.

Distracted driving (cell phone calls, texting, eating, and drinking) also causes accidents. SADD reports that the risk of a teen driving accident goes up with every added teen passenger due to distractions. Teen accidents with injuries are more likely to happen at night. Therefore, SADD recommends that parents:

- Restrict driving hours, especially between midnight, and 5 am.
- Limit the number of passengers to no more than one teen.

Your experience:

If you've had incidents of impaired driving before, then you have the most relevant experience for this issue. You can talk about any cautions or lessons learned. But I also encourage you to think back to your early driving experiences whether impairment was involved or not. Do you remember your first times riding with a peer, or driving with a friend or sibling with you? Do you remember any car accidents you've been in (including minor ones)? Think about the thoughts and emotions involved in those experiences and use those to connect with current situations. How will the driver be feeling? (Anxious? Upset? Lost? Confused? Showing off? Trying to make an impression? Under pressure? Angry? Focused?) Is the purpose of the drive something with a high potential for distraction, or to/from somewhere that likely has alcohol (e.g., a party)? That knowledge can help you anticipate situations that might need additional caution.

Signs of being too impaired to drive:

First, if somebody has been drinking at all, they probably shouldn't drive. Even a little alcohol can affect decision-making. If your son or daughter is out with friends and want to check if somebody might be unsafe to drive, here are some signs to look for that were developed by a DUI legal defense office (but shouldn't be taken as legal advice):

- Changes in how they are talking to you can indicate being impaired, including:
  o Slurred speech.
  o Talking faster.
  o Speaking louder.
  o Being unable to remember what you were talking about a moment ago.
- You might notice impairment by how someone is moving, such as:
  o Lack of balance.
  o Slow reaction time.
  o Unable to touch their finger to their nose.
  o Unable to walk straight.
- There are a couple of things that you can do with a smartphone to help assess the situation as well:

  o A company called BACtrack (**https://www.bactrack.com/**) specializes in personal breathalyzers ranging from $20-50. There is even an upgraded version that links with iPhone called BACtrack View that could help parents get verified Blood Alcohol Concentration (BAC) results remotely. That one is pricey, at $100 per month of service, in addition to the $100 breathalyzer. However, if someone is at risk of getting an accident or DUI conviction which could cost thousands, it might be worth the investment.

- ○ There is an Android app called DUI kNOw that analyzes speech patterns to check for signs of being drunk (**https://sites.google.com/site/duiknow/**).
- ○ Finally, watching your friend try to play a driving game or some other action game that requires quick reaction times can give you a sense of how they are thinking compared to usual.

What to do:

Talk with your son or daughter about their experiences related to driving with friends. It doesn't have to focus on alcohol or drugs. Make it about helping them make safe and healthy decisions. Plan ahead and discuss options for different scenarios. For example, if you or another trusted adult could help drive when your son, daughter, or friend needs help then that's probably the best. Is there a safe space where they can sober up? When those are not options, consider a taxi, Uber, Lyft, or a similar service.

You can also help your community on this issue through SADD. They work using local chapters with the goal of directly engaging students in prevention efforts. While engaged in awareness and education activities, youth also have the opportunity for leadership development. There are SADD chapters in all 50 states in the US, but even more student and school engagement would be beneficial. The organization depends on adults to volunteer as chapter advisors. **Consider getting involved.**

Answer 11: Know the warning signs for suicide

Why I picked it:

In previous chapters, I focused on the aftermath of suicide (Answer 2), and suicide risk (Answer 7), and in parallel with the increasing risk status of characters in the show, this chapter focuses on more short-term or "imminent" risk.

Primary resource:

Next year (2018), The American Association of Suicidology (AAS; **http://www.suicidology.org/**) will have its 50th anniversary as a world leader in understanding and preventing suicide. AAS is where the science of suicide interacts with clinical intervention, crisis services, community education, and prevention. In full disclosure, I'm also Chair of the Attempt Survivor and Lived Experience membership division of AAS and have been a member of the organization for 20 years.

Terminology:

- **Suicidal ideation** means thinking about or contemplating suicide.
- **Imminent risk** means immediate, short-term, acute risk for attempting suicide.

How common is suicide risk?

According to the National Survey on Drug Use and Health (NSDUH, **https://www.samhsa.gov/samhsa-data-outcomes-quality/major-data-collections/reports-detailed-tables-2015-NSDUH**):

- In 2015, 4% of US adults – 9.8 million people over 18 years old – considered suicide within the past year.
- An estimated 2.7 million adults made a suicide plan (1.1%), and 1.4 million made a suicide attempt (0.6%).
- Young adults (ages 18 – 25 years old) were the age group with the highest rates of suicidal ideation and suicide attempts.

Help is available. The National Suicide Prevention Lifeline (the Lifeline) is a national network of more than 160 local crisis centers linked through a central number (800-273-TALK) that is available 24/7 (see **https://suicidepreventionlifeline.org/**). Lifeline centers answer more than 1.5 million calls each year. (Additional disclosure: I'm also a long-time supporter of the Lifeline and Co-Chair of their Consumer Survivor Committee).

Effects of suicidal ideation and behavior include:

- Injury, severe disability, coma, or death following a suicide attempt.
- Decreased ability to function at school, or work.
- Increased stress in personal relationships.
- Increased social isolation.

Understanding suicidal ideation and behavior:

It's a myth that suicides happen with no warnings. Most teens who are suicidal communicate their distress, or even specifically talk about suicide to at least one person. Most of the time it's not with a direct statement though, so knowing the warning signs is key.

It's a myth that teens who are suicidal are just overreacting to life events. Suicidal behavior is based on individual perception. How someone sees things (i.e., if it is a "big deal" or not) is most important in determining how they will act.

It's a myth that suicide is an act of revenge or aggression. Most people who die by suicide felt like a burden to the people around them, and many believed that others would be "better off without them."

It's a myth that talking to teens about suicide will make them more likely to become suicidal. Talking about suicide honestly gives teens the opportunity to express thoughts and feelings they may have been hiding.

Ed Shneidman (suicide prevention pioneer and founder of AAS) said that the suicidal mind is filled with intense suffering and unbearable emotional pain, a struggle to see past that pain to any hopeful future, but also ambivalence. There is a conflict between wanting to die and wanting to live, and there are ways for us to help people who are suicidal to choose life.

Your experience:

If you have ever considered suicide, then you know how that depth of despair and pain feels. I'm glad that you made it through that crisis point, and if it ever gets that severe again, then I hope you will reach out to someone, or call the Lifeline. If you've never been suicidal, then I'm thankful for that, and I hope you never experience it. To help you get closer to understanding how it feels, imagine the worst feelings you've ever experienced, and then what it would be like if it seemed like the pain was never going to stop.

I'm emphasizing the feelings (again) because it is a point of connection between experiences that can be separated from details about time, place, and circumstances. Suicidal behavior is driven by powerful emotions. So, when you are considering someone's emotional state with empathy, it will help your intuition about the situation. Plus, when you are trying to connect at that level, your sincere care and concern are more likely to shine through.

Warning signs of suicide risk:

The American Association of Suicidology and National Center for the Prevention of Youth Suicide pulled together a group of experts including (among others) representatives from SAVE, Trevor Project, and AFSP to form a consensus list of warning signs indicating heightened suicide risk for youth. A teen may be considering suicide if he or she is:

- Talking about suicide or making a suicide plan.
- Saying (writing) about the future as hopeless.
- Expressing severe distress and emotional pain.
- Withdrawing from his or her social circle.
- Spending significantly more or less time sleeping.
- Showing unusually intense or reactive anger and hostility.
- Becoming increasingly irritable or agitated.

Note that AAS also has warning signs that would apply to adults such as increasing substance use, expressing a feeling of being trapped, increasing risk activities, and dramatic mood changes.

What to do:

If your teen, or one of their friends, is showing some of these warning signs, then what can you do next?

1. Ask if he or she has been thinking about suicide. Use the actual word "suicide" or "killing yourself." These questions will not put the idea into their head, but it will get you a more direct answer than you would get by dancing around your concerns.
2. Tell them about what you've observed and that you're concerned about them.
3. Listen carefully to their feelings and withhold judgment.

4. Reflect back to them what you understand about how they're doing and what's going on for them.
5. Let them know that they are not alone.
6. Let them know that some supports and treatments can help.
7. Assist them with connecting to support.

You can call the Lifeline for help 24/7, and a trained crisis phone counselor can help with assessing risk and planning next steps. As the consensus panel agreed, **"there is hope, and there is help**."

The Lifeline also offers these tips for talking with someone who may be suicidal:

- Speak in an open, honest, and direct way.
- Allow the person to express his or her feelings.
- Avoid lecturing or debating about whether suicide is "right or wrong" or how much life "should be worth."
- Be engaged and show how much you care.
- Don't dare someone to try to kill himself or herself.
- Try to remain calm and not shocked or appalled.
- Don't agree to keep it a secret, get support.
- Don't offer vague reassurance, but express your sincere belief that you will be able to find alternative solutions.
- Remove the planned suicide method (gun, pills).
- Get help from professional supports.

Answer 12: Help after rape

Why I picked it:

This episode focuses on the sexual assault of another girl by the same perpetrator as in Episode 9. As with the prior incident, **there is a graphic depiction of the second rape as well**. Since it becomes clear that the character's behavior is a pattern, the topic of this chapter concerns rape as a crime.

Primary resource:

The Rape, Abuse & Incest National Network (RAINN; **https://www.rainn.org/**) has helped over 2.5 million people since 1994 and is probably the most recognized name in addressing the issue of rape.

Terminology:

What's the difference between sexual assault and rape?
Sexual assault, also called sexual violence, is a broad term that includes all types of sexual contact or behavior without explicit consent. Thus, sexual assault includes rape, but also unwanted sexual touching, stalking, and attempted rape for example. Rape is a legal term that involves sexual penetration without consent. All rape is sexual assault, but not all sexual assault qualifies as "rape."

How common is rape?

- Approximately 30,000 cases of sexual assault and rape happen each year in the US. The rate has dropped 63% since the 1990s when nearly 70,000 cases were reported each year.
- According to RAINN, 1 out of 6 women in the US has been the victim of an attempted or completed rape (and 1 in 33 men).
- Based on Child Protective Services reports, approximately 63,000 children are sexually abused in the US each year; 2 out of 3 of those victims are between 12 to 17 years old.

Effects of rape:

- Victims of rape are ten times more likely to use major drugs (6 times more likely to use cocaine; 3 times more likely to use marijuana).
- In the two weeks after a rape, 94% of women experience symptoms of PTSD, and 30% continue to have symptoms nine months later.
- After experiencing rape, 33% of women think about suicide, and 13% make a suicide attempt.

- People who are victims of rape may also experience:
    - Problems at work or school.
    - Increased arguments with family and friends.
    - Decreased trust in others.
    - The risk of pregnancy.
    - The risk of sexually transmitted infections.

Understanding the issue of rape:

Where does rape occur? Most sexual assaults (55%) happen in or near a victim's home, some occur in or near a relative's home (12%), and some even occur on school property (8%).

Who is most likely to be targeted for rape? Regarding age, most sexual assault victims are under 30 years old, 15% are under 18 years old. Regarding gender, compared to the general population, girls between ages 16 to 19 years old are four times more likely to be the victims of sexual assault, rape, or attempted rape. Additionally, 1 in 5 Trans college students has been the victim of sexual assault. And regarding race, compared to other groups, people who are American Indian or Native American are two times as likely to be the victim of rape or sexual assault.

College appears to have some degree of protection for women but not for men. Compared to women in general, those ages 18 to 24 years old who aren't in college are four times more likely to be victims of sexual violence; while college students are three times as likely to be victims. Compared to men ages 18 to 24 years old and not in college, those who are college students are five times more likely to be the victim of rape or sexual assault.

Who are the perpetrators?

- For youth, 93% of victims know the perpetrator (59% were acquaintances, 34% were family).
- Half of the perpetrators are over 30 years old, only 15% are under 18 years old.
- For the suspected perpetrators facing criminal prosecution:
    - 37% have a prior felony conviction.
    - 10% have five, or more, prior convictions.
    - Half are released while awaiting trial by posting bail or other reasons.
    - 7% get arrested for another crime while out before trial.

Reporting of rape: Only one in three rape cases get reported to the police, and while more than half of cases that go to trial led to a felony conviction, it still ends up being less than 1% of rape cases that end in prison time.

Why people report to police:	Why people don't report to police:
- 28% want to protect a victim from further violence - 25% want to stop the pattern - 21% felt a duty to report - 17% want to catch or punish the perpetrator - 3% want to get help or recover loss - 6% gave other answers	- 20% fear retaliation - 15% don't think police will help - 13% feel it's a personal matter - 8% believe that it's not important enough to report - 8% reported to someone else - 7% don't want to get the perpetrator in trouble - 29% gave other answers

Your experience:

Please refer to Answer 9 for a more detailed discussion of this topic.

What to do:

Some discussion of sexual assault or rape may have accompanied Episode 9, and in fact, I've already provided the National Sexual Assault Hotline operated by RAINN as a suggested resource (800-656-HOPE). However, the material from RAINN presents the opportunity to discuss the topic within the framework of crime and safety.

RAINN provides some resources to help with recovery after a sexual assault, as well as for taking action in both reporting and advocacy (**https://www.rainn.org/recovering-sexual-violence**). Please know that with patient and loving support, it is possible to recover from the trauma.

For responding when someone tells you that they have experienced an assault (tips your son or daughter could also use with a friend), RAINN suggests being a good listener and using encouragement and support phrases such as:

- I'm sorry this happened.
- This must be really difficult for you.
- It's not your fault.
- I believe you.
- You're not alone.
- I'm glad that you're sharing this with me.
- You can trust me.
- This doesn't change how I think of you.

RAINN also provides information about safety and prevention (**https://www.rainn.org/safety-prevention**) that can be useful to your discussions and cover situations ranging from responding to pressure for sex to helping a friend avoid sexual assault, safety at parties, and principles for online safety. Some of the information may be useful for helping your daughter or son plan ahead for safety, and some may be helpful for them to have so that they can help their peers now and in the future (e.g., during college).

Answer 13: Seek help from school mental health professionals

Why I picked it:

First, note that this episode includes the graphic depiction of Hannah's suicide. This episode does a disservice to school mental health professionals, in my opinion, because the sole fictional representative in 13RW makes some serious mistakes and is generally ineffective.

Primary resource:

I'll note three major school mental health professional groups, but my primary recommendation is the National Association of School Psychologists (NASP; **https://www.nasponline.org/**). Admittedly, as a psychologist, I am biased on this resource recommendation. However, I was mostly convinced to select them based on their balanced and thoughtful response to 13RW (**https://www.nasponline.org/resources-and-publications/resources/school-safety-and-crisis/preventing-youth-suicide/13-reasons-why-netflix-series-considerations-for-educators**)

Terminology & How common are the school mental health professionals?

School psychologists do testing, assessments, screening, and mental health counseling. The profession requires a graduate degree or specialist training, as well as credentialing or licensure. School psychologists assist with topics ranging from special education assessments through prevention programs. NASP recommends a ratio of at least one psychologist per 1000 students for essential services or one per 500 students for more comprehensive services. School psychologists are often based at the district level providing services to more than one school.

School counselors do individual or small group sessions with students that cover a broad range of topics related to academic, career, and social/emotional development. The profession requires a Master's degree as well as certifications or licensure. School counselors assist with topics ranging from academic performance through violence prevention. The American School Counselor Association recommends a ratio of at least one counselor, in the school, per 250 students. (ASCA; **https://www.schoolcounselor.org/**)

School social workers provide help related to student social, emotional, and community needs. The profession requires a graduate degree, and certification or licensure. The social worker covers topics ranging from student crisis intervention through family assistance. The School Social Work Association of America (SSWAA; **http://www.sswaa.org/**) recommends a ratio of at least one social worker per 250 students.

Following the above guidelines, an average size high school in the United States with 750 students would, at a minimum, have access to 7 mental health professionals: one psychologist, three counselors, and three social workers. As a comparison, the high school in 13RW has just one overwhelmed counselor.

Effects of 13RW on students:

NASP says "We do not recommend that vulnerable youth, especially those who have any degree of suicidal ideation, watch this series… Its powerful storytelling may lead impressionable viewers to romanticize the choices made by the characters and/or develop revenge fantasies." They also note that the adults in the show, including the school counselor, do not portray positive and helpful actions.

Effects of comprehensive school mental health programs:

Helps promote or increase:	Helps decrease or stop:
• Communication and social skills	• Behavior problems
• Problem-solving skills	• Disciplinary referrals
• Anger management	• Suspension from school
• Crisis intervention	• Bullying and violence
• Educational performance	• Academic barriers

Understanding school mental health:

ASCA notes that 13RW illustrates the "impact and consequences when friends, parents, teachers, and school counselors aren't aware of or don't know how to intervene when a student needs help." They emphasize that counselors get specific training on recognizing warning signs, and encourage counselors to take the lead in educating teachers and parents about them as well. (See their full statement on the series here: **https://www.schoolcounselor.org/school-counselors-members/professional-development/learn-more/13-reasons-why-resources**)

ASCA underscores that ethical standards for the field may have led to a different outcome than the suicide in 13RW.

Most critically, they tell counselors:

- "Do not release a student who is a danger to self or others until the student has proper and necessary support."
- Additionally, counselors have the duty to report to parents/guardians and other appropriate authorities when there is a "perpetrated or perceived threat to [student] physical or mental well-being" as would be the case for suicide risk, as well as dating violence or sexual assault.

(Note: The ethics guidelines for psychology and social work are fundamentally the same as for counselors).

ASCA recommended that school counselors present prevention materials to classrooms along with core parts of a counseling curriculum that promote mental health. They are additionally advised to provide attention to students with mental health concerns including short-term individual counseling and community referrals to further help. Counselors are encouraged to consult with parents to help support students and work collaboratively with other school staff to identify and help students at risk for adverse behavioral health outcomes.

In guidance to the school community, NASP notes that this is an opportunity to think critically about youth problems that might be present on campus. Part of what makes the drama compelling is that the issues are real and this is a chance to take student concerns seriously. They further reinforce that practically all school mental health professionals know the errors that were made by the fictional counselor, and are trained to respond and more helpful ways.

NASP provided specific recommendations for recognizing and responding to youth warning signs of suicide risk (see Answer 11). They also noted the importance of reinforcing and promoting resiliency and protective factors. Examples include:

- Family support.
- Quality communication with parents.
- Peer support and social relationships.
- Connection to school and community.
- Healthy cultural beliefs.
- Coping and problem-solving skills.
- Positive self-esteem.
- A sense of meaning and purpose.

As a final note for school personnel, they recommend making sure that all campus spaces are monitored to promote student safety and stability.

The NASP website has reports and fact sheets related to teen issues highlighted in 13RW, including:

- Bullying
- Drug abuse
- Mental and behavioral health
- School climate
- School crime and safety
- LGBTQ / sexual minority issues

They also have a few official position statements related to themes on the show (**https://www.nasponline.org/research-and-policy/professional-positions**). Coming full circle from episode one, I specifically wanted to highlight the NASP perspective on bullying which also applies to other teen issues in 13RW as well.

"Aggression and intimidation violate the rights of students… Failure to address bullying in the school setting perpetuates an environment that is unsafe and not supportive of academic achievement, social-emotional development, and mental health. NASP believes that school psychologists are ethically obligated to ensure that all students have an equal opportunity to learn and develop an environment free from discrimination, harassment, aggression, violence, and abuse."

They encourage school psychologists to develop schoolwide prevention activities, counsel victims of bullying, assess the bullies, and provide consultation to parents of both victim and bully.

Your experience:

Did you ever see a school mental health professional as a student? What prompted it? How did it go? Depending on your experience or what you know from others, you might be inclined to defend the fictional counselor in 13RW, or perhaps you think it's "spot on." However, it's important to give the actual people at your teen's school a fair chance. Have you met them? It might be worth the effort to assess the available resources, particularly if there are any concerns about your son or daughter, their friends, or the overall school climate.

I'm not saying that all mental health professionals are great. Honestly, some aren't. That's true for any field. Parents can be powerful advocates and help change things for the better. Does the school have enough mental health staff available? Do they have a suicide prevention policy? Have they received quality training about topics that concern you? School mental health programs can accomplish a lot, but sometimes we as parents need to encourage district or administrative support for those programs.

What to do:

Has your son or daughter interacted with school mental health services? What were their impressions? If things are going well, then consider sending a thank you note to the staff. I can guarantee it would be very well received and may help keep them engaged at the school and doing good work. If there are things that could be better, then note the specifics and set up a meeting with the school mental health staff. You might end up improving things for many kids at the school. If any of the topics in this book have come up as an issue, then the school psychologist, counselor, or social worker might be key partners in getting help.

Cheat Sheet: Key resource sites and phone numbers

- **Suicide Prevention**
    - National Suicide Prevention Lifeline: Available 24/7 at 800-273-TALK (8255)
    - Suicide Awareness/Voices of Education (SAVE; **https://www.save.org/**)
    - American Foundation for Suicide Prevention (AFSP; **https://afsp.org/**)
    - American Association of Suicidology (AAS; **http://www.suicidology.org/**)

- **StopBullying.gov** for bullying prevention

- Mental Health America (MHA): mental health screening - **http://www.mentalhealthamerica.net/**

- National Center for Victims of Crime (NCVC; **https://victimsofcrime.org/**):
    - Victim Connect Resource Center (855-4-VICTIM)

- The Trevor Project: LGBTQ supports (**http://www.thetrevorproject.org/**):
    - Trevor Lifeline: 866-488-7386. Available 24/7

- Partnership for Drug-Free Kids: substance abuse information (**http://drugfree.org/**):
    - Parents Helpline: 855-DRUGFRE Available M-F, 9 am to 5 pm Eastern.
- **Sexual Violence**
    - National Sexual Violence Resource Center: (NSVRC; **http://www.nsvrc.org/**)
    - National Domestic Violence Hotline (NDVH): Available 24/7 at 800-799-7233. For teens: **LoveIsRespect.org** available 24/7 at 866-331-9474
    - Rape, Abuse & Incest National Network (RAINN; **https://www.rainn.org/**)

About the Author

DeQuincy Lezine, Ph.D., is a suicide attempt survivor who has been active in suicide prevention since 1996, including roles in the development of national and state suicide prevention plans. He received his Ph.D. in Clinical Psychology from UCLA and completed a post-doctoral fellowship at the University of Rochester focused on public health approaches to suicide prevention. Dr. Lezine is the Chair of the Attempt Survivor and Lived Experience Division of AAS and Co-Chair of the Consumer Survivor Subcommittee for the National Suicide Prevention Lifeline. He is also a member of the Suicide Attempt Survivors Task Force and the Impact Group for the National Action Alliance for Suicide Prevention, and the primary writer of The Way Forward: Pathways to Hope, Recovery, and Wellness with Insights from Lived Experience released in July 2014. He has also worked with organizations including Suicide Prevention Action Network (SPAN) USA, Organization for Attempters and Survivors in Interfaith Services (OASSIS), National Alliance for the Mentally Ill (NAMI), and the Oklahoma Suicide Prevention Council. Dr. Lezine is also author of the book Eight Stories Up: An Adolescent Chooses Hope Over Suicide (Oxford University Press, 2008). He is also the loving daddy of Benjamin and Nina (pictured with him above).

45964790R00056

Made in the USA
Middletown, DE
18 July 2017